TOP FACTS
100

DINOSAURS

Tyrannosaurus rex

The name Tyrannosaurus rex (say **tie-ran-o-sore-us**) or T rex means 'king of lizards'. The first part of its name comes from the Greek words for **'tyrant lizard'** and **'rex'** is from the Latin word for 'king'.

A T rex skeleton had about **200** bones, about the same number as humans, but they were MUCH BIGGER. Some bones had **holes** in them, to make the body lighter, and easier to move around.

Meat-eating dinosaurs like T rex are called **theropods.**

Scientists believe T rex could eat up to **230kg/500lbs** of flesh in one **BIG** bite! That's about the same weight as 100 chickens.

Its long, heavy tail was made up of **SMALL BONES** called vertebrae.

T rex weighed about the same as 2 elephants!

T rex was a fierce hunter that hunted, killed and **ate** other dinosaurs, and probably preyed on **weak** and **sick** animals.

T rex had 2 small, short front **ARMS**, each with 2 clawed **FINGERS**. It was a long stretch from its arms to its mouth!

How **fast** was T rex? Some experts say it was slow, and waddled like a duck. Others say it could run as fast as a car travels, **40kph/25mph.**

One of the **largest dinosaur teeth** ever found was that of a T rex. It was **30cm/1ft long.** Use a ruler to see just how big that is!

T rex had 2 hind (back) legs, and **walked on its toes.** It had **3 clawed toes** at the front of each foot, and **a small one** at the back.

Dinosaurs were **reptiles** (cold-blooded animals) but they **DID NOT LOOK** like the reptiles on Earth today, which include **crocodiles**, **turtles** and **snakes.**

It lived in river valleys covered in forests of trees in what is now the **western part of North America.**

T rex lived during what scientists call the **Cretaceous** period, about **66 MILLION YEARS** ago.

Triceratops

LARGE HERDS of Triceratops probably lived together, moving from place to place to find FOOD.

The name Triceratops (say **try-sera-tops**) comes from the Greek language.
tri (3) + keratops (horned face) = triceratops (3-horned face)

Triceratops lived in the forests and marshes of **western North America.**

The first FOSSILS (dinosaur bones preserved as rock) were found in 1887 in Colorado, USA. Triceratops is the **STATE DINOSAUR** of **Wyoming.**

Triceratops was not a hunter and did not need to move fast to catch prey. It moved quite **s-l-o-w-l-y** at about 16kph/10mph.

The fossil skeleton of **Triceratops Cliff** is on show at Boston Museum of Science, USA. **Cliff** cost **1 million dollars (about £700,000)!**

DANGER!
The head frill was used to **communicate** (talk) to other Triceratops and as a **warning signal.**

A large **HEAD FRILL** (a flap of tough skin) covered its neck like body armour. It protected against bites from predators like **T rex** and **Spinosaurus**, and in fights with other Triceratops. It was also protected by thick hide (skin).

Triceratops was a **herbivore**, a plant eater. It may have **knocked down trees** to get to the leaves.

Triceratops lived about **65 million** years ago.

Triceratops was about the size of an ELEPHANT, up to **9m/30ft long**, and **3m/10ft tall**. It weighed about **6 tonnes/7 tons**.

Triceratops had **3 horns** on its head. 2 'brow' horns above the eyes were about **1m/3ft long** and made of solid bone. A shorter horn on the snout (nose) was not bone, more like a **big fingernail**.

Triceratops had up to **800 teeth** – but not all at the same time! Arranged in groups, as some teeth wore out they were **replaced by others**. It had a mouth shaped like a **parrot's beak**, for pulling and crushing plants like ferns and palms.

Triceratops needed big legs to carry its **huge body**. Its fore (front) limbs (legs) were shorter than its rear (back) legs. It had **3 hooves** on its fore limbs and **4 hooves** on its rear limbs.

The **HUGE** head of Triceratops was one third the size (about 33%) of its whole body. SKULLS have been found that measure **2.5m/8ft**.

Pterosaurs
Flying Reptiles

Could dinosaurs fly? NO! Pterosaurs (say ter-o-saws) did fly, but they were FLYING REPTILES, not dinosaurs. Pterosaur means 'winged lizard'.

Most Pterosaur **skulls** were full of tiny teeth, like sharp needles, but some had no teeth at all!

Pterosaur bones were not solid (like dinosaur bones). They were hollow (empty) and filled with air sacs (pockets). **WHY?** It made them light enough to lift their bodies into the air.

Most Pterosaurs had back-facing, cone-shaped head crests. What were they for? Displaying (showing off) to find a **mate**? Controlling the direction of their **flight**? Experts are not sure!

Pterosaurs did not have wings with **feathers**. Some had wings made of muscle and skin stretched between the VERY **l-o-n-g** 4th finger of their 'hand' and their back limb (leg).

Were Pterosaurs the first creatures to **fly?** NO - insects were the first.

Flying kept Pterosaurs **safe** from predators (hunters) but some were caught. How do we know? A Pterosaur fossil bone had a dinosaur tooth in it!

Pterosaurs **flapped** their wings but also used the wind to **GLIDE** through the air, using less energy.

Pterosaurs were carnivores (meat eaters). Most ate **fish**, flying low over rivers and seas to catch them in their **long, narrow jaws**. Some had throat 'pouches' (pockets) for scooping up fish, like today's pelicans. On land they ate **insects** and **dead animals**.

Pterosaurs were NOT designed for **walking**, and were **clumsy** on land.

Quetzalcoatlus (say kwet-zal-co-at-lus) may be the largest creature EVER TO FLY. It measured about 15m/50ft from one wing tip to the other, and its head was the size of a small **CAR!**

Pterosaurs lived in **North** and **South America**, and parts of **Europe** and **Asia** about 200 MILLION years ago.

Pteranodon (say ter-an-o-don) had **3 fingers** on the front of each wing, and short back legs.

Dinosaur limbs (legs) were under their bodies. Pterosaur limbs stuck out from their sides, like lizards and crocodiles.

Pteranodon Café
MENU
fish
dead dinosaur bits
crabs
insects

Iguanodon

Iguanodon (say **ig-wah-no-don**) was a herbivore, a plant-eating dinosaur. It lived about **125 MILLION** years ago on mainland Europe and in England, North America and Africa.

A great discovery was made near a coal mine in **Belgium** in 1878 — the fossil bones of more than **30 Iguanodons!**

Iguanodon was **large** and **bulky**, not built for speed. But its size made smaller meat eaters less likely to attack it.

How big is big?
Iguanodon's front limb was about the size of a man and it weighed about as much as a van!

Iguanodon had a **sharp spike** for a thumb and used it to stab leaves and open seeds. It may have used it to **stab** hunters that wanted to eat it, too!

★ TOP FACTS

IGUANO-FACTS

How long?	about **10m/30ft**
How heavy?	about **3 tonnes/3 tons**
How fast?	about **20kph/12mph**

Iguanodons laid **eggs** on land, sometimes buried in sand. **Babies** hatched out, like **birds**.

What we know about dinosaurs can change. We first thought Iguanodons walked on all **4 limbs**, then that they walked on **2 back limbs**. In fact, they may have walked on **2 OR 4 limbs!**

Some people think **Iguanodon** had **83 teeth!**

Adult humans have **32!**

thumb!

When **experts** first found Iguanodon **fossil bones** they built the skeleton with the **thumb spike** on the NOSE!

Iguanodon had a very long **5th finger**. It used it to gather plant food like **leaves**, **shoots** and **twigs**.

Iguanodons had powerful back limbs (legs) and shorter front ones, with small hooves. Each foot had **3 toes**.

Iguanodons may have lived in **herds** (groups). Why do we think this? Because lots of **skeletons** have been found together in **one place.** Living in herds protected them from **hunters**.

Chewing tough plants all day was hard on Iguanodon **teeth!** As they wore out they were **replaced** one by one by new ones.

Diplodocus

DIPLODOCUS (say **dip-lod-ic-us**) was a dinosaur called a sauropod. It lived in the western part of North America about 150 MILLION years ago.

Dinosaurs lived **millions of years ago**, but we have only known about them for about the last **200** years, since the 1820s.

Diplodocus was about 30m/100ft long. Its neck measured **6m/20ft** and its tail was EVEN **L-O-N-G-E-R**, with about **80 bones**! That's longer than a **bus**!

Diplodocus's brain may have been just **10cm/4ins** long! It MAY have had a 'second brain', a swelling near the base of its tail that helped **control** it.

Diplodocus swallowed stones that stayed in its stomach. They helped to grind the hard leaves it ate into a softer **pulp**.

Diplodocus lived on land, in groups called **herds**, but could wade through water in lakes and rivers to find FOOD.

Diplodocus had **5 toes** on each foot and **1 large claw** on the first toe of each back foot.

Diplodocus may have been the **l-o-n-g-e-s-t** dinosaur measured head to tail. We know this because skeletons have been found and measured. Other dinosaurs may have been longer, but we cannot be sure as **no complete skeletons** have been found.

Diplodocus ate plants and trees like **mosses, ferns, cycads, gingkoes and conifers**.

Thwack!
Diplodocus may have used its tail as a **weapon**.

Because it was a herbivore **(a plant eater)** Diplodocus's little 'peg' teeth were all at the front of its mouth, to rip leaves from plants. It had no back teeth because it did not chew meat. Its teeth may have lasted for only about a month!

Diplodocus was slim and light (about **10-12 tonnes/11-13 tons**) compared to other dinosaurs. **Brachiosaurus** weighed about TWICE as much!

Fossils of Diplodocus were first found in Colorado, USA, in 1877. They have also been found in the states of **Montana** and **Utah**.

Fossil **footprints** left in mud tell us that Diplodocus walked on **4 big feet**, a bit like an elephant. It moved quite s-l-o-w-l-y at about **8kph/5mph**, but could move faster if it was in danger.

Plesiosaurs
Water Reptiles

Plesiosaurs (say ples-i-a-saws) were water reptiles that lived on Earth about 65 million years ago. They swam in both **fresh water** in lakes and rivers, and in **salt water** in seas and oceans.

Some **Plesiosaurs** were only about **3m/10ft long.**

Elasmosaurus (say **ee-laz-mo-saw-rus**) was a Plesiosaur. It was about **14m/45ft long** and weighed about **2 tonnes/2 tons.**

The first **Elasmosaurus** fossils found were VERY different from anything seen before! When experts fitted the skeleton together they put its head on the end of its **tail!**

Each of Elasmosaurus's 4 paddle-shaped flippers may have been about the size of a **man!**

Elasmosaurus's **l-o-n-g** neck was half of its whole length and had about **70 bones** in it!

Plesiosaurs swam under water to **hunt for food.** They had strong jaws, and ate bony fish, and animals like today's water snails, squid and octopus.

Parts of a skeleton were the **first Plesiosaur fossils** (remains) found in England in 1719.

Question:
Did Plesiosaurs walk on land?
Answer:
NO!
Because they had flippers, not legs, they **DID NOT** walk on land.

The **huge** bodies of Plesiosaurs helped keep them safe from attack. So did their **sharp teeth!**

There are 2 kinds of Plesiosaur:

True Plesiosaur
long neck, small head

Pliosaur
shorter neck, large head

★ TOP FACTS
Some people believe these 'monsters' are Plesiosaurs still living in lakes and lochs!

name	place
Nessie	Loch Ness, Scotland
Champ	Lake Champlain, North America
Ogopogo	Lake Okanagan, Canada

Nessie?

Plesiosaurs had a broad body, a short tail, and **4 swimming flippers** instead of limbs (legs).

Plesiosaurs **MAY** have laid eggs in sand at the water's edge, like today's **turtles.**

Stegosaurus

Stegosaurus (say **steg-uh-saw-rus**) was a large dinosaur that lived in the **Late Jurassic** period about 150 MILLION years ago.

Stegosaurus's **TAIL SPIKES** were up to **1m/3ft long.** Some had **2 sets of 2 spikes**, and some had more.

Stegosaurus had a HUGE body but a TINY brain. It may have been as small as a golf ball!

★ TOP FACTS
As BIG AS A BUS! Stegosaurus was:
- about **9m/30ft** long
- about **3m/10ft** tall
- about **5 tonnes/5.5 tons** in weight

Stegosaurus is the STATE DINOSAUR of Colorado, USA. The first fossils were found there in **1877**.

Stegosaurus lived in **herds** (groups) of both young and old animals. It was SAFER than living alone.

Plant eaters like Stegosaurus **did not have to run** to catch food. Large and **bulky**, it probably walked slowly, at around **7kph/4mph.**

ANTI-ATTACK!
Stegosaurus's size may have put off hunters like Allosaurus. So might its bony back plate armour, and slaps from its spiky tail!

Stegosaurus may have **swallowed stones**. In its stomach their rough edges helped **break up** the tough leaves it ate.

Othniel Marsh found the first Stegosaurus fossils. The bony back plates made him think of roof tiles, so he gave it a name from 2 Greek words:
stegos (roofed) + saurus (lizard) = stegosaurus

Stegosaurus had about **17** bony '**plates**' called SCUTES along its back. The largest measured **60cm/2ft** and may have been for display (showing off).

At the front of its mouth Stegosaurus had a '**beak**' - but no teeth! Its teeth were in its cheeks, and it used them for chewing.

Different kinds of Stegosaurus have been found in **Europe** (in **Portugal**), **China** and **Africa**.

Stegosaurus was a **herbivore** that ate forest plants and trees like mosses, horsetails and conifers. Did Stegosaurus eat grass? **NO** - grass DID NOT EXIST at that time!

Stegosaurus may have been able to **lift itself up** on to its **back legs** to reach leaves on tall trees.

Quiz

Try answering these questions to test your **TOP FACT 100** info intake.

Answers below.

1 Did Iguanodon eat PLANTS or MEAT?

2 Which dinosaur's brain may have been as small as a **golf ball?**

3 Which **dinosaur** name means **'king of lizards'?**

4 How many **horns** did Triceratops have on its head?

a 1

b 2

c 3

5 Pterosaurs could fly. **True** or **False?**

6 This is the **outline** of **which** dinosaur?

7 Use the **clues** to name the dinosaur.

a   I was a plant eater.

b   I may have had 83 teeth.

c   I was as heavy as a van.

8 Is it true that a **T rex tooth** measured 30cm/1ft?

10 Which of these things could Plesiosaurs do?

a   walk on land

b   swim

c   fly

9 The first Triceratops **fossils** (bones) were found in which country in 1887?

TOP FACT

100

NATURAL WONDERS

Mountains

MOUNTAINS are made when parts of Earth's crust are forced UP as high as **8km/5 miles**. Some are **still growing!**

A range is a GROUP of mountains.
The **Himalayas** in Asia is the HIGHEST range.

FACT 1: 25 million years old
FACT 2: has 30 of the highest mountains

WORLD'S TALLEST MOUNTAINS:

1 EVEREST
China and Nepal
8848m/29,030ft

2 K2
Pakistan and China
8611m/28,250ft

MOUNTAIN ANIMALS ARE ...

LIFE IN THE HIMALAYAS

8000m/26,000ft **nothing can live**

6700m/22,000ft
tiny **jumping spiders** eat flies blown up by wind

4000m/13,000ft
marmots **hibernate** (sleep) for 8 months a year

HUNTERS
puma
snow leopard
spectacled bear

GRAZERS
ibex
yak
chamoix

★ TOP FACTS

CONTINENT	MOUNTAIN	HEIGHT
Africa	**Kilimanjaro**	5895m/19,340ft
Europe	**Elbrus**	5642m/18,500ft
Antarctica	**Vinson Massif**	4892m/16,050ft

The ANDES in South America is the L-O-N-G-E-S-T range, 3 times LONGER than the Himalayas.

Some mountains are
VOLCANOES

1 PLATES (pieces of Earth's crust) **press together.**

2 Inside Earth, MAGMA (HOT liquid rock) and GASES build up.

3 They ERUPT (explode) through openings.

4 When magma cools down it becomes hard LAVA.

★ 3 TOP FACTS

★ Earth's **atmosphere** was made from gases from volcanoes.

★ **Eruptions** can send hot ASH **30km/17 miles** into the air.

★ There are **200** active volcanoes in the Andes.

IN SPACE ...

MAAT MONS is a volcano on the planet Venus **6km/4 miles high**.

IO, one of **JUPITER's** moons, is covered in volcanoes.

OLYMPUS MONS, on Mars, is 3 times **HIGHER** than Mount Everest.

The island of **Hawaii** is the peaks of **5 undersea volcanoes**. MAUNA LOA (long mountain) has probably been erupting for 100,000+ years. It is **100km/60 miles long X 50km/30 miles wide**.

Question:
What is the **Ring of Fire?**

Answer:
A ribbon of land and water **40,000km/25,000 miles** long with **450+** volcanoes.

FUJIYAMA,
an active volcano,
is **Japan's** highest mountain:
3776m/12,390ft.

ACTIVE volcanoes ...
may erupt

DORMANT volcanoes ...
have not erupted for 10,000 years, but may erupt again

EXTINCT volcanoes ...
will never erupt again

In Yellowstone, USA, **ROCK** is heated by **SUPER-HOT MAGMA**. The rock heats RAIN and water, and **GEYSERS** shoot BOILING WATER and STEAM **100m/330ft** up into the air.

Rivers

A RIVER is a body of **fresh water** on land that flows into a sea, lake, or other river.

The **AMAZON** has **more water in it** than the **next 7 longest rivers added together!** It takes water at least a MONTH to flow from the Andes to the Atlantic Ocean.

★ TOP FACTS

Some rivers are **very short.** The Roe river in Montana, USA, is **61m/200ft long.**

3 **longest** rivers:

Nile	Africa
Amazon	South America
Yangtze	China

People don't agree on which is l-o-n-g-e-s-t. It depends where they are measured from.

FACT! The top 3 are all at least 6400km/4000 miles L-O-N-G.

A BASIN is land a river takes water from. The Amazon basin is the largest. It covers almost **HALF of South America**, about **7 million square km/2.7million square miles.**

The Chinese name for the YANGTZE is CHANGJIANG, which means **long river.**

Russia's **Ob** is the largest river to **FREEZE SOLID** in winter.

The Nile got its name from the Greek word for river - NEILOS. An **underground** river that flows below it has **6 times more water** in it.

Rivers **start small**, and get water from **rain, snow, ice and land.** The FORCE (power) of water wears away earth and rock, making **VALLEYS** and **CANYONS** (deep cuts).

The Colorado River carved the GRAND CANYON in Arizona, USA, over **6 million years.**

★ average depth? **1.6km/1 mile**   ★ average width? **16km/10 miles**

Question:
Where is the LARGEST CANYON?

Answer: On the planet MARS. **Valles Marineris** is up to **8km/5 miles deep.**

FACT: On Earth it would **start** at Los Angeles and **end** at New York!

The largest canyon on Earth may be **under Antarctic ice.** It could be **1000km/620 miles** long.

When river water flows over **tall ledges of rock** it makes WATERFALLS.

ANGEL FALLS,
Venezuela
TALLEST:
3 times as tall as France's Eiffel Tower

VICTORIA FALLS,
Zimbabwe
Spray and mist 30m/100ft high

IGUAZU FALLS,
Argentina
275-300 separate waterfalls

People have gone over **Niagara Falls,** between the USA and Canada, in boats and barrels - and in 1859 Charles Blondin walked across on a TIGHTROPE.

★ TOP FACTS

LAKES are large bodies of water with **land around them.**

LAKE	LOCATION	TOP FACT
Baikal	**Russia**	DEEPEST, over **1600m/5250ft**
Tanganyika	**Africa**	LONGEST, **673km/420 miles**
Dead Sea	**Israel, Jordan**	LOWEST point on Earth, 10 times saltier than sea water

The USA's 5 GREAT LAKES are the **largest GROUP of lakes,** with **over 20%** of the world's fresh water.

Deserts

Deserts are **dry, flat, empty places** that cover about 20% of land on Earth.

Deserts get less than **25cm/10ins** of RAIN a year.
Most places get at least 4 times as much.
About 20% of deserts are covered in SAND, and some are **rocky.**

Plants, **animals** and **people** live in deserts. They ADAPT (change) to live there.

PLANTS like **cacti** need little water.

The ADDAX ANTELOPE gets **water** from grasses and leaves it eats.

KANGAROO RATS eat their own **poo** to get water!

Over 1 BILLION PEOPLE live in deserts. Some **move around** with their animals, and live in tents.

The Sahara Desert is g-r-o-w-i-n-g. Trees are **cut down**, animals like goats **eat plants,** and there are DROUGHTS (times without rain). RESULT? **More land** becomes **DESERT.**

HOT DESERTS are ...

super HOT in the day

super COLD at night

Temperatures in the largest HOT DESERT, the Sahara, can be **up to 49°C/120°F.** It takes **7 DAYS** to drive across.

450 million years ago ... Africa's SAHARA DESERT was covered in ICE.

About 6000 years ago ... plants and trees grew there, eaten by **giraffes** and **elephants.**

Some deserts have SAND DUNES shaped by winds.

Sand dunes in the Sahara can be **180m/600ft high.**

Issaouane Erg is a **sand sea** in Algeria. The sand can be **30m/100ft deep.**

Question:
What is an OASIS?

Answer:
A place in a desert where there is **WATER**.

Rocks in **Monument Valley,** USA, were shaped as water WORE AWAY SOFT SAND over millions of years. This left tall shapes with flat tops and straight sides, called **mesas, buttes** and **spires.**

Death Valley is the **lowest, driest** and **hottest place** in the USA.
HOT FACT!
Highest temperature is **57°C/134°F!**

South America's **Atacama Desert** is the DRIEST place on Earth. **4 years** can pass without rain.

DESERT FACT 1!
There are LAKES in deserts, some under the ground.

DESERT FACT 2!
There are HILLS, bare rock with straight sides.

Some deserts are COLD. The largest **cold desert** is in Antarctica. It is a desert because it is DRY. Parts of the Arctic and Antarctica NOT COVERED IN ICE are called **polar deserts.**

The **Great Victoria,** Australia's largest desert, is home to **rock wallabies, parrots** and **snakes.**

CAMELS can go without water for days. They **sweat very little,** so do not lose moisture.

★ KEEPING COOL!

★ Small animals **rest in burrows** or under stones in the day, and come out at night.

★ Some snakes **bury themselves in sand.**

★ **Fennec foxes** lose HEAT through HUGE ears.

★ Some lizards **lift each foot** off hot sand in turn.

Oceans

The **SALTY** waters of OCEANS and SEAS cover over 70% of the surface of Earth.

There are **5 OCEANS.** They hold about **96.5%** of all Earth's **WATER.**

In winter **ICE** about **50m/160ft deep** covers the **ARCTIC OCEAN.** WHALES, **seals** and **jellyfish** live in its icy waters.

The SOUTHERN OCEAN around Antarctica is covered in **ICE** ALL YEAR ROUND. **Emperor penguins** live on the ice, where it can be as cold as **-60°C/-76°F.** Brrrr!

About 70% of the OXYGEN we **breathe** is made by oceans.

Oceans affect **weather** and **temperature.** They support an amazing variety of **LIFE**, from tiny animals called **krill**, to huge **whales**.

★ TOP FACTS

1 The PACIFIC OCEAN is the **largest** and **deepest,** and covers over 30% of Earth's surface.

2 The ATLANTIC OCEAN is about half the size of the Pacific, and is still **g-r-o-w-i-n-g.**

3 The INDIAN OCEAN is more than **5 times the size of the USA!**

4 The ARCTIC OCEAN is at the **TOP** of Earth.

5 The SOUTHERN OCEAN is at the **BOTTOM** of Earth.

We have explored less than **5%** of the **black** and **cold** D-E-E-P-E-S-T ocean waters.

SEAS are **smaller** and **shallower (less deep)** than oceans.

Arabian   Baltic   **Caribbean**   Coral   **Mediterranean**   North

Can you name any other SEAS?

The **Sargasso Sea** in the Atlantic is the only SEA without a **SHORE** (land border). It is **deep blue,** and full of floating mats of **seaweed**. **EELS** go there to **lay their eggs.**

More than HALF of Hawaii's **Mauna Kea** mountain is **under the sea.** Measured from the sea bed, it is **taller than Everest.**

MOUNTAINS

TRENCH

SEA BED

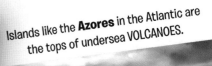

Islands like the **Azores** in the Atlantic are the tops of undersea VOLCANOES.

WAVES are caused by **WINDS** blowing over ocean waters. The **stronger** the wind, the **BIGGER** the wave.

TRENCHES are long, narrow cuts in the ocean floor. The **deepest** we know about, the MARIANA TRENCH, is **11km/7 miles down. Challenger Deep** may be the **lowest point** on Earth.

★ TOP 3 FACTS

UNDER WATER there are ...

★ **flat plains** about **6km/4 miles** below the surface

★ **mountains** called SEAMOUNTS

★ the world's **longest** mountain range, the Mid Ocean Ridge is **65,000km/40,000 miles** long

Twice every day, the level of water in oceans and seas RISES and FALLS. These changes are called TIDES, and they are caused by the **MOON.**

When the Moon is overhead it PULLS water towards it.

Question:
What is a TSUNAMI?

Answer:
A **HUGE** wave caused by **earthquakes,** or erupting volcanoes.

Caves

CAVES are **natural holes** or gaps in hillsides, rocks, ice - or under the ground.

There are CAVES in glaciers (rivers of ice) ...

... and in **lava**, the hardened MAGMA that has erupted from volcanoes.

Caves can be small holes, or huge spaces called **ROOMS**, **CHAMBERS** or **CAVERNS**. They are dark and damp because they get little or no LIGHT and HEAT from the SUN.

Caves are made when ACID in WATER **dissolves** (wears away) soft rock like **limestone**, making holes. This can take **MILLIONS** of years.

★ TOP FACTS

LONGEST
MAMMOTH CAVE in Kentucky, USA, is the **longest NETWORK** of caves: 652km/405 miles of tunnels and caverns.

DEEPEST
KRUBERA CAVE, in Georgia, is the **DEEPEST CAVE** we know about, more than **2km/1.2 miles deep.**

People who **explore caves** are called CAVERS or POTHOLERS. Cave divers visit underground rivers and lakes.

Water that drips to cave floors has a mineral called CALCITE in it. Very slowly, this **builds UP** to make tall, slim shapes called STALAGMITES.

STALACTITES take hundreds of years to **GROW DOWN** from the cave roof.

FACT!
If a STALACTITE and a STALAGMITE **join up,** they make a PILLAR.

The first people used caves as **SHELTERS**. Ones at **Lascaux** in France have DRAWINGS that were scratched and painted on the walls about 17,000 years ago.

Australia's **JENOLAN CAVES** are the **oldest** we know about. How old? **About 340 million years.**

An EYE (hole) in the roof of a cave near Lagoa in **Portugal** is **16m/52ft across.**

Fingal's Cave, on the island of Staffa in Scotland, is a sea cave **70m/230ft deep.** Tall pillars of a rock called BASALT have **1 2 3 4 5 6 SIDES.**

FACT! BEARS, **BATS** and **BIRDS** use caves to shelter in.

At **low tide**, when the sea is shallow, people walk to SEA CAVES at Canada's **Bay of Fundy.** At **high tide** the caves fill with water.

There are **streams** and **waterfalls** in the Waitomo Caves, New Zealand. Roofs are lit up by thousands of tiny insects called **GLOW WORMS.**

FACT! Some fish and insects that LIVE in dark caves have: NO COLOUR X NO EYES X

Meteor Crater is a huge BOWL shape in the Arizona Desert, USA, nearly **1.6km/1 mile across.** It was made about 50,000 years ago when a **meteorite** (a huge rock from space) smashed into Earth.

Where land and sea meet, the **power of waves** wears away soft rock to form steep SEA CLIFFS.

Bright white cliffs at Dover, England, are made of **CHALK.** They formed 100 to 70 million years ago.

Ice

12% of Earth is always covered in SNOW and ICE.

Tall mountains are so cold that when SNOW falls, it **never melts**. More snow presses down, making a hard ICE CAP on the tops, and rivers of ICE called **GLACIERS** flow down the sides.

ICE CAPS can be **60m/200ft thick**. The Antarctic ice cap has **70%** of the world's fresh water.

FACT!
There are VOLCANOES under the ICE CAP in Norway.

At the **TOP** and **BOTTOM** of Earth, the Arctic and Antarctica, it is so cold that glaciers and frozen ICE **do not melt**. They move to the sea **super s-l-o-w-l-y**, and CALVE (break up) into pieces of floating ice called **ICEBERGS**.

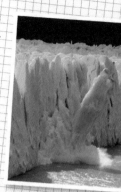

GLACIERS form over **thousands** of years. The Karakorum mountains in Pakistan and India have many of the largest.

Some icebergs are so **TALL** (**1km/0.6 mile**) that they get STUCK ON THE SEA BED, and break up.

FACT!
450 million years ago, what is now the **Sahara Desert** was covered in GLACIERS.

Antarctic icebergs are LARGER than Arctic ones.

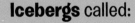

ANTARCTIC

ARCTIC

Icebergs called:

★ **GROWLERS** are the size of a small CAR

★ **BERGY BITS** are the size of a small HOUSE

One of the biggest ICEBERGS, **B-15**, broke off an ice shelf in Antarctica in 2000. **SIZE? About 295km/183miles long x 37km/23miles wide.**

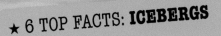

★ 6 TOP FACTS: ICEBERGS

1 More than 90% are in **Antarctica**.

2 About 15,000 break off in the **Arctic** each year.

3 Most Antarctic bergs last about **10 years**, Arctic ones **2 years**.

4 Iceberg ice is a lot HARDER than freezer ice.

5 Icebergs are safe to eat because they are made of FRESH WATER.

6 Icebergs can drift around for years, but MELT in **warm waters.**

1 million years ago, a deep ICE SHEET covered about 33% of Earth. When it melted, the level of the sea ROSE, and deep valleys made by glaciers **FILLED WITH SEA WATER.** Norway has many of these FJORDS.

What we see is only about 10% of an iceberg: **90% is under water**.

GREENLAND's ice sheet covers 80% of the whole island.

Scientists collect ICE from icebergs. Some ice is **800,000 years old**, because that's how long it can take glaciers to form. BUBBLES in the ice have **very old AIR** in them.

Some **midges**, FLEAS and **ice worms** live on icebergs. Birds visit to eat them.

FLOES are large, flat pieces of SEA ICE. Some female SEALS give birth to their **pups** (babies) on ice floes.

ADELIE PENGUINS hunt small fish that live on the underside of ice floes.

Wonders

Man has made many amazing things. But they cannot match the **WONDERS** made by **NATURE**.

The **GREAT BARRIER REEF**, in the Coral Sea, off Australia, is the world's LARGEST CORAL REEF system.

South America's PANTANAL is a huge WETLAND. The water can rise by **5m/16ft**, and some parts are always under water. Plants like lilies and hyacinths grow there.

LIVE corals get their colours from **algae** (sea plants) that grow on them.

CORAL: THE FACTS

Tiny animals called **polyps** build SKELETONS shaped like CUPS around themselves. When they **DIE,** skeletons pile up and make a CORAL REEF (ridge). This takes **MILLIONS** of years.

DEAD coral is **white.**

The EVERGLADES wetlands and swamps, in Florida, USA, are home to the **manatee,** a gentle plant eater that feeds on seagrass.

RAIN FORESTS cover 2% of Earth's land, but have 80% of its life. Different animals live in 4 **layers** of the AMAZON rain forest:

1. EMERGENT
tops of tallest trees
harpy eagle   butterfly

2. CANOPY
leaves and branches of most trees
monkey   toucan

3. UNDERSTORY
trees, shrubs, vines
boa   jaguar

4. FOREST FLOOR
dark, damp ground
ant   frog

Northern Ireland's **Giant's Causeway** is about 40,000 columns of BASALT rock. Most have 6 SIDES, but some have **5 7** or **8**.

Lac Rose in Senegal is a PINK lake.

The River of Five Colours in Colombia has
1. RED plants 2. GREEN sand
3. YELLOW sand   4. BLUE water
5. BLACK rock

ULURU (Ayers Rock) is a sandstone rock in Australia **3.6km/2.2 miles long, 1.9km/1.2 miles wide.** As the Sun sets it changes from **brown** to **orange** to **red**.

The AURORA BOREALIS (northern lights) are **waves of colour** that 'dance' across the skies.

The round PADS (leaves) of the Victoria **water lily** float on water, and can measure up to **3m/10ft across.** Its white FLOWERS turn pink, and can be up to **40cm/ 16ins across.**

The Monteverde Cloud Forest in Costa Rica is covered in **mist** and **clouds**. More than 750 kinds of TREES grow there.

The Salar de Uyuni in Bolivia is the **largest** SALT FLAT. Shapes with 6 sides form on a crust of WHITE SALT up to **10m/30ft deep.**

Question:
Tallest tree?
Answer:
California's REDWOOD. One called Hyperion is **116m/380ft tall.**

Karlu Karlu (the Devil's Marbles) in Australia are huge red, ROUND GRANITE BOULDERS up to **6m/20ft across.** Some balance on top of others.

More than 15% of EVERY kind **of plant** grow in the **Amazon cloud forest.**

Question:
Largest flower?
Answer:
RAFFLESIA ARNOLDII. Up to **1m/3ft across,** it smells AWFUL!

Quiz

Try answering these questions to test your **TOP FACT 100** info intake. **Answers below.**

3 Would you see **STALAGMITES** and **STALACTITES** in a cave or river?

1

What is the name of the world's TALLEST MOUNTAIN?

2 GROWLERS and BERGY BITS are kinds of what?

A iceberg

B river

C volcano

5

Which of these is **NOT** a river?

a Nile

b Amazon

c K2

4

The **SAHARA** is a DESERT.

true ✔ or **false** ✗

6

Maat Mons is a volcano on which **PLANET?**

7

The **canopy** and **understory** are 2 layers of what kind of forest?

8

In which country is **ULURU** (AYERS ROCK)?

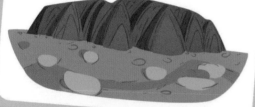

9

Is the **ATLANTIC** the largest ocean?

yes ✔ or **no ✗**

10

How much of an **ICEBERG** is **ABOVE** the water?

a 10%

b 50%

c 90%

37305418R00023

Printed in Poland
by Amazon Fulfillment
Poland Sp. z o.o., Wrocław